Potpourri

by Graham Harrop

ISBN-13: 978-1535513029
ISBN-10: 1535513020

Made from a tree
That looks quite a fright
This crocodile timber
Is more bark than bite

Towelephant

This delightful creature
will keep you dry in all kinds
of weather
and will
never
forget
to
empty
the
laundry
hamper

grahamharrop.com

Slithery Sid sidles along

Singing his slithery snake

singing song

The Jumping Crickenhopper

Known for its
ability to jump,
this tiny
invertebrate
has won its
share of
gold
at the
insect games

grahamharrop.com

A master of disguise, Albert would ultimately be caught and sent back to Leavenworth prison, where he would, ironically, face the music

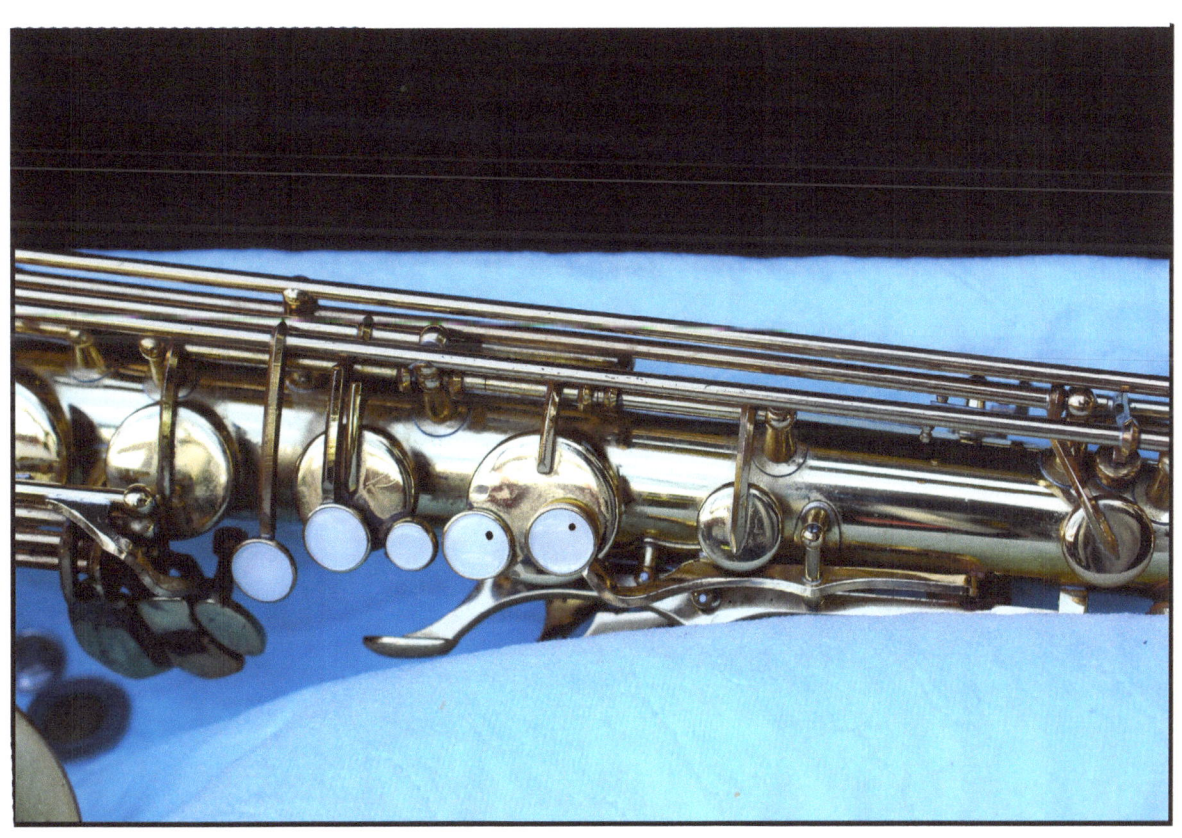

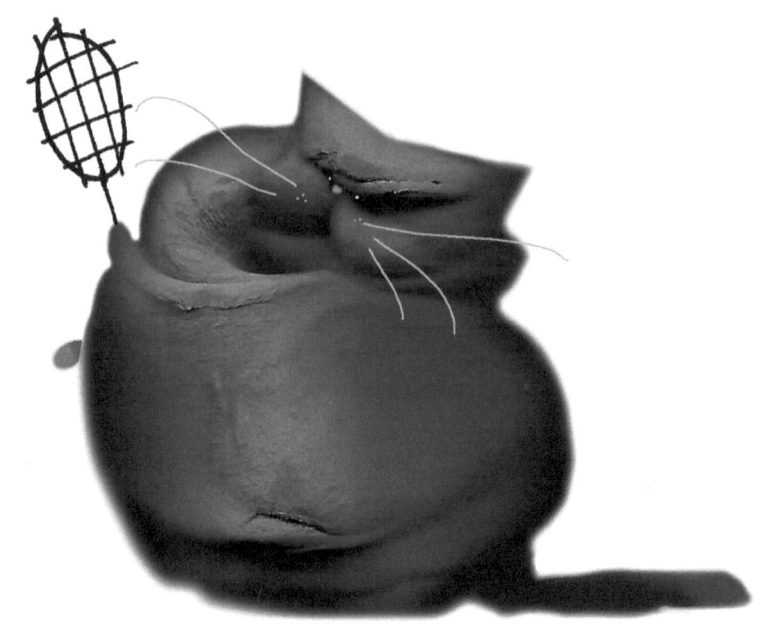

Made from erasers
Which make him look fat
This badminton kitty
Is a real putty cat

Norman was a dog who loved grilled cheese.

His mother said: *'Don't eat too much or you will turn into a grilled cheese sandwich!'* And he did

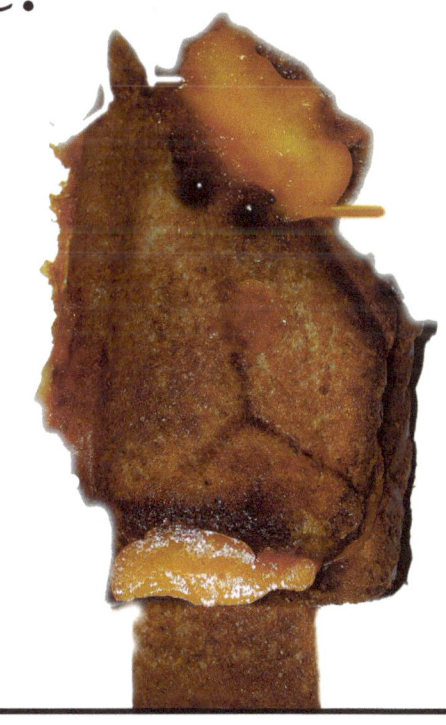

© grahamharrop.com

With a roar
and a growl
Some patience
and practice
A little
brown twig
becomes
Vertabractus

grahamharrop.com

Made from a cloth that's used to wash dishes

A sad little bluebird has fly-away wishes

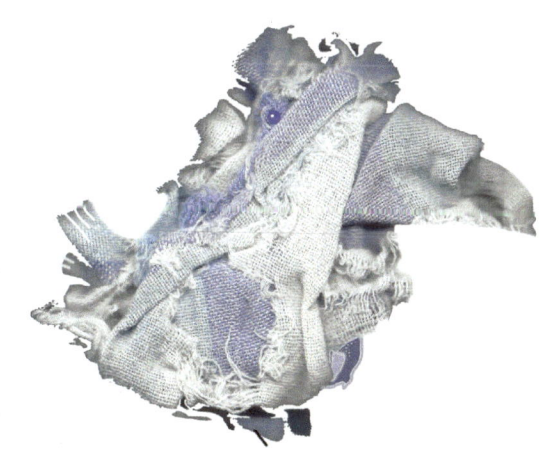

Calling themselves the Pea-tles,
Fred, Norm, Wally, Ed and Earl
attempt to replicate the famous
walk across Abbey Road.

Golden retriever uses his
dog collar to lasso owner
and

negotiate
a new
contract

The bird who thought he was a canary

Wallace was a 300 pound bird who thought he was a canary, One day somebody said: *'Get a grip!'*

and that was
the end of that!

Japanese lady hides in
poppy's gentle bloom

dreams
of the
warm
soil

Silently stalking his prey,
Ed, an autumn-leafed rat,
suddenly hears the loud
ringing of his cellphone,

Through plastic and waste
That keep out the rain
This small sad-eyed creature
Seeks shelter again

The Krooner bird croons and has petals for wings. Songs about sunflowers are all that he sings

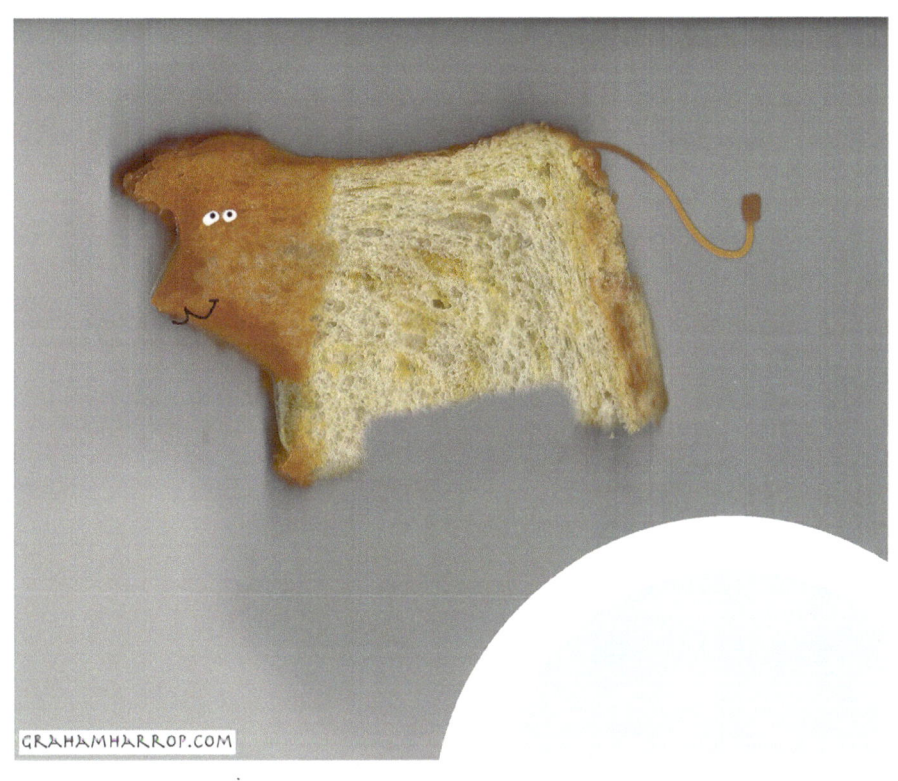

Ready for breakfast
At the marmalade spread
This calico cow
Is just so well-bread

Birds on a wire

Honestly, Mavis - I don't know
how she can fly aound in an
outfit like that! Last year's
crest! Tacky topknot!
And that plumage!
My goodness!

Magnolia Horndrake
Serves at the store
Raspberry rhinos
Are never a bore

© grahamharrop.com

Chlorophyl parrot Ever so practical Beak made for swinging Feet zygodactical

As evening falls
and tiny lights
appear, a small
blue finch
thinks about
making his
way back
home.

Rabbit was left
On industrial site
Indignant dust bunny
Troublesome plight

Lost in woods
hears a sound
bramble-haired leafenhound

© grahamharrop.com

Blanky Bird
Avis Blankus

A member of the Fliederdown family, this rare and comforing bird has a tendency to roost on bedposts and coo small children to sleep

Green leaf frog leaps
onto stage in attempt
to enter show business

GRAHAMHARROP.COM

Orange peel goldfish

Squeezed in a bowl

Swimming in circles

Has taken its toll

X-ray proves a trifle embarassing for small bird who is not used to being seen without all of his feathers on.

Curious little creature wonders if he can join children playing hopscotch in the schoolyard.

Carl was never very comfortable in front of the camera, and now down here at **the police station** the feeling was even more **intense**

Two-button creature
Terrycloth shirt
Is terribly nervous
of late
Too many times he's been
washed and spun dry
And left in a terrible state

Philisophical French bird
thinks: 'An oeuf is an oeuf!'

TOAST CRUMB DUCK
DISAPPEARS INTO
THE MORNING MIST

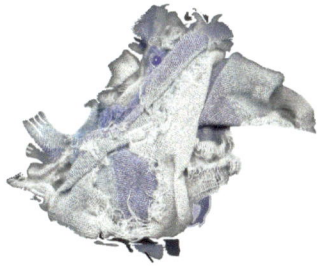

from GryndstoneandFusspotPress.com

www.ingramcontent.com/pod-product-compliance
Lightning Source LLC
Chambersburg PA
CBHW040308010626
45792CB00025B/1477